How To Set Up A (Successful) Dance Class In 6 Easy Steps

A.D. Padgett
(M.A., P.G.C.E.)

Published by
Dancing Detectives

First Published 2010
Copyright Anthony Padgett 2010

ISBN 978-0-9561587-7-2

DISCLAIMER: Reading this book and applying its principles will in no way guarantee a successful dance class and the author accepts no responsibility for any classes that are not a success. No resemblance to any actual persons living or dead is intended in this work

How To Set Up A (Successful) Dance Class In 6 Easy Steps

A.D. Padgett
(M.A., P.G.C.E.)

Dedicated to STS
and to all the kind and lovely people that
we have had the pleasure to meet and teach.

THE 6 STEPS

STEP 1 – Geographical Location

STEP 2 – The Venue

STEP 3 – The Equipment

STEP 4 - Advertising

STEP 5 – Your Classes

STEP 6 – Staying Successful

6

INDEX

INTRODUCTION   p 11

Are You Good Enough?
Do You Teach Beginners Or Advanced?

STEP 1 – GEOGRAPHICAL LOCATION   p 19

Before Setting Up
Market Research
Collaborations

STEP 2 – THE VENUE   p 23

How To Find A Venue
Features Of A Good Venue
    1. Good Visibility
    2. Dance-floor Status
    1+2. Feeder Venues
    3. Cost & Big Or Small
    4. Parking
    5. Heat And Ventilation
    6. Good Lighting
Availability
Approaching The Venue
Negotiating Costs
Timing Of Setting Up The Class
Sample Letter Of Agreement

STEP 3 – THE EQUIPMENT   p 37

a) Music
b) Music System
c) Lighting
d) Venue Decoration
e) Seating Area & Ventilation
f) Drinks
g) Visitors Book
h) Takings Book
i) Public Liability Insurance
j) CRB
k) Professional Qualifications

STEP 4 – ADVERTISING   p 47

Creating A Brand & Logo
Physical Advertising (Flyers, Posters, Banners etc)
Advertising In The Electronic Media (Websites, Facebook etc)
Advertising In The Physical Media
Press Releases
Press Release Template
Publicity Photographs
Copyright Of Other Peoples Images
Permissions For Putting Images Of Dancers On-Line

STEP 5 – YOUR CLASSES   p 57

Dance Partners
Do You Teach Beginners Or Advanced?

Setting Up A Beginners Class
Setting Up An Advanced Class
Price
Teaching Attitude & Tone Of The Class
Dancing In The Middle With Partner
Vs Dancing With Students
Encouraging Couples To Move Around
Bonding With Customers
Core Dancers
Goal Setting
Program Of Dance Moves
Youtube Movies
Dancing Demonstrations
Congresses & Being The Best
Competitions
Open Air Events
Weddings
Holidays
LESSON TEMPLATE

STEP 6 – STAYING SUCCESSFUL   p 75

Being A Success May Be The Start Of Your Problems
Staying One Step Ahead
The Psychology Of Dancers
Dirty Tricks
    Negativity
    Undermining Students
    Poaching Customers
    Gazumping
Knowing When To Quit

APPENDIX p 89

POSTER/ FLYER/BANNER TEMPLATE

A-FRAME (OUTSIDE VENUE) TEMPLATE

WEBSITE TEMPLATE

SAMPLE PRESS RELEASE

INTRODUCTION

So you want to be a dance teacher? Or you want to set up a dance class? Or you already have a class and want to pick up a few extra tips on making it as great a success as it can be? Here's a non-exhaustive manual of how to set up Salsa and Swing dance classes without the need for an expensive qualification.

Following this book does not guarantee that your class will be a success, and your class may be a success even if you don't follow it, but it will definitely help you maximise your chances of being successful if you apply yourself to the principles in here. It is not a rigid blueprint and circumstances vary between situations and personalities.

However, for the price of a couple of lessons you now have 7 years of insight into setting up and running dance classes.

REMEMBER- Different people have different definitions of what success is. Personally I define it as maximising your potential and the potential of those around you in a positive environment of mutual support and respect. What it is not is seeking to deliberately impede the success of others through inconsiderateness, impoliteness, negativity or aggressiveness. Try defining your own idea of what a successful dance class would be so that you can set your own goals and know when you have achieved success.

Your reasons for setting up can be many – there is no one teaching within 10 miles – you want to start a small informal group – you would like an extra income stream and to use your new dance skills – your local class is overflowing and the teacher is too busy to put on an extra night - you think your area could be socially regenerated with a dance class to help people get fit, make friends, lose weight and stay off alcohol and drugs.

Whatever the reasons, unless you are an extremely confident person you will no doubt be asking yourself the next question.

Are You Good Enough?

The first thing that you need to know is that to be good enough you don't need an expensive dance teacher's qualification. The formalisation of dance teaching came about after the evolution of the dance styles. In business the process is described as forming, storming, norming and performing. And that's what happened with dance. Different people would approach a dance in different ways, each saying they had the correct way, until an authoritative body was established that said what the correct way to dance was.

Some people need to follow authority and a single, definitive style. But as long as you have the basically correct way of teaching you will be fine. And as long as you teach basic moves from one or more of the original strands of dance then you will be correct.

I waited 10 years before having the confidence to start teaching only to find people setting up around me after a year of my teaching them. As they evolved the moves they taught completely changed, and each time they claimed that they had the best way of dancing. So it is also important not to make unjustified claims about the "correctness" of your teaching. The main thing is to check that you are teaching the generally correct moves so that your customers are getting value for money.

To find the correct moves and ways of teaching you can go to a few different classes. Write down a list of the key moves that you would like to include in a class, this will also help you get the names of the moves (although names may vary between teachers). Also watch what how the teachers teach, and work out how you would teach the moves yourself. Each person evolves their own teaching style.

Don't worry about your ability to teach as your classes will probably start off small and you will probably be with friends or with people keen to learn who are more nervous than you are. They will be able to give you tips and advice about what they think works best. Just keep at it, follow the program in STEP 5 - YOUR CLASSES and things will evolve.

Besides, whenever you get students new to dance then they will not know if you get the teaching wrong, so relax and build your confidence and style. As you see people developing and becoming able to dance then your confidence will grow.

The second thing that you need to know is that you don't have to be the best dancer in the world. Great dancers are not always great teachers. All you need is to be good enough at dancing and as you start teaching you will gradually find out if you are good enough to teach in the eyes of your customers.

To begin with, you need to have the basics and at least 10 good dance moves and want to start a dance class.

Don't be anxious to show your customers that you are a great dancer if you don't feel confident about your teaching. Stay focussed on what will work most effectively for their learning. People can't take in too much information, so just aim to give them 1 or 2 new moves each week or fortnight. Include familiar moves so that they are comfortable and aim that everyone gets the moves to encourage a sense of achievement, confidence and belonging in your dancers. After a couple of months if no one has been able to learn anything from you then it may be time to think of a different job/hobby.

Do You Teach Beginners Or Advanced?

By the time you have a group of dancers who can do the basics then you will have probably gained more difficult moves to show them (if you didn't have them already) and you can develop as a group with the better dancers helping those with less experience. You can augment your learning with DVDs and Youtube lessons and research the history and various styles of the dance of Wikipedia and other online sources.

At this point you may wish to begin a more advanced class. Or you may have set your heart on teaching a small advanced class from the start. Either way you will need to decide on this because as your classes develop some people begin to take the dancing very seriously and develop arrogant and supercilious airs (becoming what are termed dance snobs e.g. "salsa snobs" or "swing snobs"). Do not worry about them. They will soon leave.

If you want to keep these people then it is the "treat them mean, keep them keen" mentality that you must adopt. Don't care if they can't follow the lessons, just put all the blame on them and not on yourself. However, to run this kind of a class needs to be parasitic on there already being a successful beginners class in your area (your own or someone else's) so that your class can be seen as inspirational to the arrogant dance snobs. This book is not aimed at those kinds of dancers or teachers.

They seem to have an attitude like one that Groucho Marx joked "I don't care to belong to a club that accepts people like me as members." Woody Allen adapted this into not wanting a girlfriend that would want someone like him as a boyfriend and the same psychology applies to dancers. Some dancers seem to think "I wouldn't want to go to a dance class that I could actually do." They do not thank teachers for making it easy for them to get the moves so that they can remember them, rather they feel under challenged and develop an air of superiority (even thought they could not do the move before you taught it to them).

They gravitate towards teachers who have arrogance about their dancing (as if it somehow made them a better person) and who like to teach difficult moves in their classes. This can be to show off but can also be because they want their students to struggle so that they don't learn the moves and become better dancers than themselves or good enough at dancing to become teachers.

Thankfully there are not many people like this (at least not to begin with). How you relate to them is discussed in STEP 6 - STAYING SUCCESSFUL.

The point is that you will need to be aware of them and your decision on whether to set up a beginners or advanced class should be made after considering all the points in STEPS 1-6. These STEPS are of different lengths but each is of near equal importance.

REMEMBER: Having a successful dance class is not about being the best dancer, that's subjective and there are plenty of people who are deluded about their own abilities and selective in what they see in other dancers so that they can continue their self-delusion. The same with groups of dancers and teachers. They can decide to boycott you even though you are a better dancer and teacher.

Don't expect the dance scene to be reasonable. It is great when it is (and you should always be reasonable yourself) but other dance teachers can be envious and want to create a climate of dislike of you and your class to further their own egos and dance classes.

REMEMBER: The best dancer in an area might also be the best teacher even though they just teach beginners.

Having a successful dance class is about being the best teacher and this is not just how well you teach your students. Rest assured, many of the principles needed for this are contained in the following pages.

STEP 1 - GEOGRAPHICAL LOCATION

Before Setting Up

Some key features to consider before setting up a dance class are the catchment area, the population density and dance culture within that area. When we began in a provincial town 6 years ago there was no teaching of and no interest in adult recreational dancing and a distinct prejudice towards men dancing. Consequently it took us 2 years to build up to a regular class of 20-40, a number that took us 2 months to reach when we set up in a city with a culture of recreational dancing.

Market Research

Market Research is not the same as advertising. Marketing is about finding out who your potential customers are so that you can design a product to meet their needs. Market led means that you provide the dance form that the customer wants, so if everyone wants Morris Dancing then you teach Morris Dancing. Product led means that you teach what you want the customer to learn regardless of what they do want to learn. However, advertising can also change desires for dance forms within the market place.

So find out what people in the area are interested in and you might be able to harness that interest into another dance form. So you can get people to come to a Morris Dance lesson and then introduce them to Salsa or Swing dancing. Or hold your Salsa dancing in a Tapas bar where the market is already interested in Latin culture because of an interest in Spanish food.

REMEMBER: Do not try and change people too much. It is better to be just half a step ahead than a full step ahead. If the market is really not likely to be interested in your dancing then you might be better starting up somewhere else.

To carry out your Market Research then try to answer these questions:

How large is your catchment area? Which geographical area are you catering for? How far are you prepared to travel (as travel adds time and expense to your weekly class)?

Is there a Market for your dancing in that area? i.e. establish that there is a market. It will be an uphill struggle if you try starting in an area where no one wants to learn how to dance.

How many dance classes are in the area and how well is that market currently being provided for? Which other teachers are in the area? Are their classes busy or quiet?

What kinds of dancing are being done? Is your favourite dance catered for? Are there already too many classes? Are there lots of beginners in need of an advanced class? Are there lots of advanced classes with no one teaching beginners?

Do you need to start completely from scratch as there are no dance classes in the style you want to teach? If this is the case then try and work out why there are no dance classes. Did someone start and fail? If so then what did previous teachers do wrong?

Finally, you can decide if you can add a class to the area or whether it would be better to go further a-field?

Collaborations

If there are other teachers in the area then contact them before setting up. Listen to their concerns and work together with them if you can. Avoid setting up on the same night in the same area just because you might want to go to dance classes out of town on the other nights. Offer to set up on a different night to show that you are reasonable. Most of all respect all their hard work and remember the maxim "do as you would be done by". Also if you tell them that you will put flyers in your class you build up good will between you, them and your customers.

Try to work with other dance teachers on joint projects, harmonising dance styles. You can work together by being guest teachers in each others events. Bring students from your classes to their events and they can reciprocate.

If you start off on the right foot then approaching joint projects will be a lot easier. Don't feel bashful about approaching other teachers because you feel you might offend them by setting up. As long as you aim to generate your own customers and not take theirs then you should not let fear stop you talking with them. They will appreciate your honesty, sincerity, respect and manners.

An analogy for teachers working together is countries trading together in the global economy. If there is protectionism and trade restrictions then the global economy will slow down like it did in the Great Depression in the 1930's and people won't trade with each other. Eventually you will get conflicts and a dance war. This environment of infighting, bickering and rival factions will stop people wanting to learn to dance. However, some teachers thrive in this environment (due to their aggressive personalities - as did the weapons manufacturers in the Second World War) so be careful of these teachers as they are not interested in cooperation. Even when you want to work together they just want to compete.

If teachers don't reciprocate then find teachers who will and be wary of setting up in an area where there is aggressive competition.

STEP 2 - THE VENUE

Now that you have decided on an area you will need to find a venue that will host your dance class. Possible venues for dance classes are bars, hotels, nightclubs, working men's clubs, church halls and town halls.

The great advantages of running a dance class out of other people's venues is that they are easy to set up and you don't have all the overheads (of lighting, heating, tax etc). The downside is that you are not in full control of your class – which means that there can be double bookings, cancellations, venue closings and changes in management.

Don't worry about the downsides at the moment. What you need to do in the first instance is to create a list of venues. The most important thing you will need to do as a dance teacher is find a good venue. It can't be stressed how important this is as if you get this right at the start it will save all kinds of problems at a later date. Don't rush into setting up. Take your time to get the best venue. Plan with a view to expansion if you get busy. If you don't plan this then someone else probably will as soon as you start to get busy. Don't expect any loyalty from your students. It may be one of them that sets up against you and gets the benefit of all your hard work.

The more systematically you approach this the better and easier it will be. You may start your classes only to find out a year later that a much better venue is just around the corner (or just 10 miles down the road) and one of your students has decided to set up in competition with you.

REMEMBER: A teacher is only as good as their venue in the eyes of the customer. This is because the teacher is the provider of a number of factor for the customer, so if you don't provide the best venue, then, in at least one factor, you are not as good a teacher as another teacher who does provide a good venue.

How To Find A Venue

You may know of a venue that you think will be ideal for your class but before you commit take a little time to look around.

Search the internet and make a map. Find a search engine such as Google or Yahoo and type "TOWN NAME" and "dance-floor" or "venue for hire" or "working men's club" etc. Use the inverted commas as this will search for the phrases. Then you can collate the results that come up for the venues and dance-floors. Try and list them into regions/areas/postcodes in the town. Give each venue a number so that you have a database of venues. Then take the postcodes for each venue and type them into Google-map and you will be able to piece together a map of all the venues in your area. Give each venue a number and then add the number to your map. Then you have a map and a list.

This gives you a good graphic way to approach visiting each venue and you can cross venues off your map and list when they are not suitable. You can also put the pros and cons of the venue on your list if you are unsure how good the venue is. Soon you might even find that your original venue is not as suitable as you first thought. And if it was as good as you thought, then you can now rest assured.

REMEMBER: Doing an online search will not give you all the venues in your area and it may also give venues that no longer exist.

It helps if a good venue is on a main road (see below). So drive down the main road and if you see a venue then stop and pop in or just peer through the window at the dance-floor. Always be on the look-out for a good venue with good visibility and good parking. This leads us to the next part...

Features Of A Good Venue

The following are listed in order of importance:

1. Good Visibility – a venue that is in a prominent position in town or on a main road is ideal as this will help you to advertise your dance class, reaching thousands of customers every day. However, there are other things to consider, such as whether the venue has space and will allow you to hang a banner, sign or A-frame outside to advertise to the passing traffic. A small poster is not sufficient. It needs to be a minimum of A2 size and larger (e.g. A1 or A0) is better.

2. Dance-floor Status - you will need a good dance floor with room for growth. A sprung wooden dance floor is best. A wooden floor that is not sprung is second best. Floors with ridges and tiles are to be avoided. Wooden floors in bars that are not regularly cleaned are also to be avoided as spilled drinks leave sticky deposits.

You may think that the floor surface will not be a problem as you can put talcum powder down to make it more slippery. However, talcum powder on the floor makes a mess for cleaners – particularly if mixed with beer – and the management may tell you not to put it down.

Sometimes you don't need to visit the venue if the venue has a website with images of the floor, parking etc. You can also do online searches about a venue and come up with images on Flikr etc of peoples' wedding events and parties at the venue.

Please note that "size really does matter". The more students that you can fit in the class the more room you will have for growth and the fewer students will leave because it is too busy. As students become more sophisticated they may seek quality (of the dance-floor) over quantity (its size) but they will still go to a class which is busy regardless of the floor's quality - as long as it meets the minimum requirement of their being able to spin and turn.

Students will also go to where a floor is not very good if the lesson is good and/or if nowhere else is providing what they want. However, if you want to keep your students then get a good floor.

REMEMBER – You may think that the dance-floor is more important than the visibility but 1 & 2 go hand in hand, and here is how…

1+2. Feeder Venues - If your venue is not good (e.g. it is a high visibility venue but the floor is too small) then it will be a feeder class for other classes (other peoples or your own). Creating a feeder class is good if you can direct the overspill of customers to a less visible class that you run that has a large floor. However if you don't have a larger venue then poachers will direct them to their classes instead.

Conversely, if you have a large venue but poor visibility then it is more difficult to generate customers and it is difficult to create atmosphere in a half empty club.

3. Cost & Big Or Small – Managers of smaller venues will often let you use them for free, however, try to avoid the temptation to take them until you have looked for a large venue, with a large wooden floor, on the main road, that has good parking and advertising opportunities. This is perfect and may also be available for a low fee (or even free). However you may need to build up class numbers for a venue if the manager requires a large hire fee.

It is not advisable to take a venue with a large fee until you know that you will be able to provide enough students to cover your costs and make a profit. Find a smaller venue where you can build up your class but have a list of the other venues to hand so that you can move into the larger venue when you need to.

If a competitor sets up in a smaller venue then remember that there will now be 2 classes to eventually feed the larger venue, so go to the larger venue before your competitor does. Arrange to move there on a date that will have given you and the competitor plenty of time to build up the dancer numbers. If you are sure that you will be able to provide enough students over time then try and make a deal with the venue to negotiate a low rate until the numbers of students pick up. Give it a time frame and put everything in writing so there is no disagreement later.

4. *Parking* – ensure that there is good parking at the venue or nearby and that it is in a safe area. The worst thing is to come out of a night dancing and find that your car has been broken into, vandalised, given a ticket, towed away or wheel clamped. A car park for a venue in a rough area is only second best, even if it has CCTV. However, without the car park then there will be psychological barriers for a number of customers.

5. *Heat And Ventilation* – you will need a venue that is not too hot in the summer. Check that there is good ventilation (windows, doors, air conditioning or fans) otherwise you may need to bring your own fans in summer. Check it has a good heating system so that it is not too cold in the winter. Some venues, like Church halls, can be too hot in winter if their heating system is geared to the elderly. So they will need windows (make sure that these can be opened and are not stuck). If you need to open windows and doors then you might also need to check about noise levels if you are in a residential area (as neighbours may complain that the noise is too loud for the night time).

6. *Good Lighting* – you will need a room that is light in the summer (so that people don't feel they are in a dungeon if the weather is nice outside) but is also capable of blocking out the light so that an atmosphere can be created. If the venue doesn't have disco lighting you may need to provide your own – see STEP 3 - THE EQUIPMENT.

Availability

By now you may have done a good deal of research about a venue before you approach the management and find out the last thing and most important thing, its availability.

There is no point finding the ideal venue if it is not available on the night that you need it. However, if it is ideal then you might think about changing what day you can teach on and if you are lucky the venue might also be flexible about its days. The more you know about the venue when you approach the management the better light it will put you in - as you have already shown a level of commitment to them by showing a level of interest in them.

Also the last thing you want to do is waste your time and the management's time by visiting venues that are not suitable.

Approaching The Venue

There should be a phone number online or on a sign outside the venue. Ring up and arrange to visit so that you can see the venue and get a feel for the management and how well you might work with them.

Some managers are warm, friendly, easy going and approachable. Other managers are hard-nosed inflexible business people who will drop you and your class at a moment's notice. They will speak as if they are fully supportive but will not arrange for the premises to be open on time or properly staffed and then treat you as a problem if you raise this with them.

Either way, it is always good to e-mail after any meeting, just to clarify that you have understood what they have said and they have understood what you have said.

The good managers will follow this agreement. So get a deal in writing in case the management changes. However, don't expect to stick too closely to it. Keep a relaxed attitude otherwise you might annoy them and they will be less likely to honour the agreement. If you are unsure how supportive the manager really is then even if you put an agreement with them into writing (e-mail or letter) there is still no guarantee that they will honour the arrangement if they are not supportive.

Managers may expect to make a lot of money off drinks sold in their bar. Don't let them build up a false expectation as by the time you have built up your class they may decide that it is not making enough money on the bar for them. Furthermore, problems can arise with venues when dancers bring their own drinks. So create a sign that says "The management politely requests that customers only consume drinks that are purchased on the premises". This will help to keep the management happy without your having to nag your dancers.

Also let the management know what the other benefits are e.g. increasing awareness of their function room facilities, creating a lively and fun atmosphere in their venue, creating positive associations for the venue within the community. Let them know that your class becomes a form of public/community relations and advertising for them – as well as your providing a revenue for them from any fee that you pay them.

Make sure that the venue is not about to close down, to refurbish or to get new management.

Negotiating Costs

Finally you need to get down to the nitty gritty. Listen to what amount they suggest. You might shoot yourself in the foot by offering £20 a week when they were about to let you have the venue for free.

If you break down your costs and time investment they will also understand you have to do more than just teach the class for 3 hours a week. This will help them understand that you are not making as much per hour as they might otherwise think.

If they want more than you can afford then an alternative is to have a period of grace (i.e. free rent) whilst establishing the class and then a scale of fees depending on how many students you get (see the "Sample Letter Of Agreement" at the end of this chapter).

Timing Of Setting Up The Class

When you approach the venue management have in mind a date when you want to begin your class. Make sure that you have plenty of time to do all the advertising (particularly if you are building a dance scene from scratch) otherwise no one will know of your new class.

The best times to set up are:

Autumn – when the schools return and parents are looking for something to do in the long winter nights.

New Year – when people want to follow a New Years resolution and want an activity for losing weight and getting fit.

The worst time to set up is:

Summer – when people are on holiday, looking after their children and enjoying long sunny evenings.

Sample Letter Of Agreement

The following is a sample letter that you might send (post, hand deliver or e-mail) after a meeting. It gives some of the areas that you might cover. You will need to fill in the information and amend the details…

YOUR ADDRESS

DATE

VENUE ADDRESS

Dear *MANAGER'S NAME*

Re: Dance Lessons At *VENUE*

I should like to put in writing my understanding of some of the arrangements that we made *DATE OF PREVIOUS MEETING* regarding the commencement of dance lessons at *VENUE*.

I understand that these are subject to adjustments and amendments by yourself. Please feel free to add/remove any of these points.

Commencement Date/Time

Weekly classes to begin on *DAY* evenings from *DATE*.

Your staff will open up at 7pm and the classes and practice dancing are to run from 7.30pm till at least 10.30pm. Your staff will then lock up the premises.

Fees

Hire Fee to commence after a 2 month period of grace whilst building the class.

After 2 months it is hoped that there will be at least 20 – 40 dancers and the Hire Fee of £X will commence for a 2 month period. If these numbers are not reached then it will be decided if it is worth continuing with the class.

After a further 2 months it is hoped that there will be at least 40+ dancers and the upper limit Hire Fee of £Y will commence. If these numbers are not reached then the lower hire Fee of £X will continue until these numbers are reached.

Payment

Payment will be by invoice and cheque, made at the end of the month to "*RECIPIENT NAME*".

Advertising

A banner or sign (provided by myself) is to be mounted at the side of the building (*or railings etc*) prior to commencement of the classes on *DATE*.

Small poster(s) (provided by myself) are to be displayed inside *VENUE*.

Use Of Facilities

We will be able to use the music and lighting system.

The bar will be open with bar staff.

The Ballroom will be set out fit for the purpose of dancing i.e. tables and chairs removed from the dance floor with enough for use by customers.

Customers will be able to use parking at the venue.

First Refusals

We are trying to create a new dance scene in *TOWN* and your *VENUE* could become a really successful for this. However dancing has become highly competitive and it is likely that once we start that you will be approached by other dance teachers. In such an eventuality then to reward our work in promoting *VENUE* as a dance venue, we appreciate if you kindly offer us first refusal on teaching another night at *VENUE*.

Yours sincerely

YOUR NAME   *MANAGER'S NAME*
(Dance Teacher)   (Manager)

STEP 3 - THE EQUIPMENT

By now you might have found a perfect venue, one that even provides you with all the equipment you will need, including a great music system and disco lighting. Don't worry if it doesn't as these are easy to provide. However, even if it has everything you will still need to provide certain other extras before you can start teaching.

You will need (in addition to the ability to dance and the knowledge of how to dance). Some items you can buy in shops or get off the internet (keep costs down by buying on e-bay). What you will need will depend on your venue and your taste. Here is a list of some of the things that you might need to purchase.

a) Music

You will need to play music that is easy to dance to. Generally speaking, it is only when dancers become really good that they distinguish between nuances in genres of music. They are more interested in being able to dance to the music and will blame you if they can't dance to the music, rather than themselves. Indeed, it is not just your job to provide the customer with music that they can dance do, but also that they want to dance to.

Only those interested in Djing and collecting music will be purists about the music – and often it is more that they are interested in what is being played in other venues rather than that they really understand the music. If this is the case then the best course of action is to ask them to bring you a copy of the music that they like or bring you the names of the music so that you can get it yourself. This will keep them happy and remove your competitors advantage of having better tracks. Play what your customers want as to survive you will need to be market led, rather than product led.

Most CDs that you buy will only have 1 or 2 good tracks, so copy these to a computer and give them names with ratings for slow, medium or fast. Copy the best slow and medium tracks onto 2 CDs to use for teaching. You will only need 1 or 2 CDs when you first start so select the very best tracks with an easy beat and also a catchy tune.

b) Music System

A laptop computer is a good way to carry around all your music. However you are unlikely to use all the tracks so you can copy the best to some CDs or put them on an MP3 player. This will give you all the tracks you need for an evening in a form that can be carried around in your pocket.

Both laptop and MP3 player will need an adaptor that will run starting from the earphone socket and ending with Red and White leads that go into the back of the music system. If you are unsure of how to switch input modes then ask the management at the venue or ask an assistant in the shop where you bought your music system.

If you need a CD player system then get a portable but loud one as you will need to carry everything in a box or be able to store the box at the venue. You can get players with built in amps but separate speakers. These usually give better sound than a 1 piece system and look more professional to the customer. Make sure you check the output as a system that is physically the same size as another system could have a lower Wattage and Ampage. Ask for advice when buying.

Your music system may need PAT electrical testing if it is not new. Some venues require this but the majority do not mention this. PAT testing can be done by an electrician for a small fee. If your items are new then they will not need to be tested but for your own safety it is a good idea, particularly if you have purchased second hand equipment. Being electrocuted or starting a fire with faulty equipment is to be avoided. When you unplug any appliances then you should always switch off at the mains socket first.

c) Lighting

A single disco light can transform a dull room and create an instant nightclub atmosphere. If the venue doesn't provide one then you can buy LED disco lights. These are less noisy than older style disco lights and the bulbs last a lot longer. Your lights may need PAT electrical testing if not new.

When you were checking the venue you would have made sure that you would be able to make the venue dark enough to use disco lights in the summer (particularly if it is a venue that needs disco lights to create a good atmosphere).

d) Venue Decoration

Some kind of decoration appropriate to the dance form can be used to create an atmosphere when you set up the room. If it is a church hall then the more you can make it feel like a night club the better. This will stop your class feeling like a class and make it more of a night out where people can practice their dancing.

The most important venue decoration is yourself and your dance partner. Dress appropriately for a night's dance class and social dancing. Get dance shoes so that you look the part.

The second most important venue decoration is your dance flyers. Put these on a table by the door. These reinforce the message that students are learning in a professional dance class and club.

A logo at the front of the room (e.g. a neon sign, an LED sign, a banner, a poster etc) can be used to reinforce your brand and also add to the dancers' experience of dancing the dance form. Make sure the logo is appropriate to the dance – e.g. red, yellow, blue or pink for Salsa and black and white for Swing.

Hanging decorations may also need to be fire tested and if you have too many decorations this will take a long time to set up. A small number of portable, easy to set up and iconic items are best for the easy creation of an atmosphere.

A movie projector can also be used to create a special event atmosphere. You can show films and music videos from a computer or DVD player connected to a data projector or a games projector. The downside is that (as well as copyright restrictions) the system takes a good deal of time to set up and needs a good deal of darkness to be effective.

The best advice is that if a venue has such a projector already set up then try and make use of it. If you set your own up then don't expect the majority of people to notice it or the work you have gone to. Do it because you want the effect and also in the knowledge that the effect it has is subliminal.

e) Seating Area & Ventilation

If you need to arrange the tables and chairs yourself then do it the same each week so that people can feel at home and familiar.

If there is poor ventilation and no air-conditioning then fans may be needed in the summer. Cheap office fans are normally available from supermarkets during the summer season. Don't buy one of these unless someone complains about the heat.

f) Drinks

An irony of dance classes is that many social dancers want a drinks area but dancers don't drink a great deal – other than cheap soft drinks. This means a lot of venues don't make a great deal on you using their facilities. Make sure the venue doesn't have false expectations about how many drinks will be sold. Their disappointment may make them decide to ask you to leave.

Watch out for a plastic bottle culture where people bring their own drinks. The dance class is not like a fitness class. It is also a social class in a drinking environment. You will annoy the management if they see people drinking soft drinks. When asking people not to bring their own drinks put it down as a management request so that they do not feel resentment towards you. A sign can be useful – for sample wording see STEP 2.

In some venues you may need to provide drinks. This is an extra job that you may not want to take on. So if you sell bottles of water and cans of fizzy drinks for twice the price that customers can get them in a shop then this will encourage people to bring their own drinks rather than rely on you for cheap drinks.

Venues with an alcohol licence will also require someone with a personal alcohol licence to be present if alcohol is to be sold. If you have one then this may be a good income stream as anyone (18+) can sell alcohol as long as 1) the venue has a licence and 2) there is a personal licence holder present. If you are putting on larger events then you may want to get an alcohol licence so that you can sell alcohol. Temporary venue licences for events can also be applied for from the local council.

g) Visitors Book

Next to the entrance door should be a table for your Visitors book (and flyers) where you can take e-mail addresses and comments. Have a good quality book as it values both your class and your customer's comments.

Arrive early so that you can set up and welcome all the dancers and get them to sign the book. You may not have chance later.

h) Takings Book

You will need to keep a list of takings each week. Don't use numbers in the class as sometimes people will forget to pay or will avoid paying. Just keep a record of the amount that you receive. Deduct the venue hire fee and any expenditures from you business to get your yearly taxable amount.

i) Public Liability Insurance

This is absolutely necessary when teaching. Search online for a cheap insurer and if you can't get public liability insurance specifically as a dance teacher some firms let you get covered under the category of fitness instructor.

Regardless of this, make sure that the dance floor is safe, with no sharp edges of tables and bars near to the dance area. Also make sure that you have a word with any dancer who is a danger to other dancers. If they remain a danger then you may need to request that they leave (otherwise you may lose dancers).

You may also get some customers coming to you who do not appear to be fit to dance. Ask them for a Doctor's note of permission if you are concerned. If they refuse to bring you one then make sure that you ask them in your partner's presence so that you have a witness. Tell them that they dance at their own risk and you might also want to get them to sign a letter saying that you have asked them for a Doctor's note and that they dance at their own risk.

j) CRB

This is necessary if working with Children. The new legislation, as I understand it, will require a dance teacher to have Criminal Records Bureau (CRB) check for any teaching with children. However, if you teach only 18+ then this is not required and so saves an additional cost.

k) Professional Qualifications

These are not necessary at time of print. Don't let dance teachers make you think that you must pay them to take one. Similarly, don't let professional dance associations/alliances make you think that it is necessary to become one of their standardised fee paying teachers. This may help in stopping them teaming up against you if you are more successful than they are (though there is no guarantee of that).

The most useful thing about a qualification is that you can use it to advertise your qualification to reassure dancers. Unscrupulous teachers might also use their qualification to criticise other teachers without one. This goes in the dirty tricks section as unfortunately, in my experience, professional dance organisations do not always seem to teach against doing this in their business ethics.

New legislation (when it does come in and it seems to be perennially delayed) will make accommodation for people who have already been working as dance teachers. Those who have experience will not need to also get a qualification. Furthermore, the requirements for a qualification will only apply to those who want to work in publicly funded organisations. Private organisations such as private clubs, hotels and sport centres, will have their own policies on this but I have never been asked for a qualification by either public or private organisations.

If you need to put your qualifications in a letter, or on your website, then any relevant higher qualifications (such as a degree in dance or a postgraduate certificate in education) are useful to site. You may also add if you have a BA, BSc, MA, PhD etc and any teaching qualification e.g. PGCE, is also useful to site. However, previous experience as a dance teacher is the most useful quality to refer to.

So, instead of spending time and money on getting dance qualifications you might want to save your money for insurance and setting up. Qualification can be like a pyramid scheme where teachers with qualifications can go on to teach other dancers to become teachers. A qualification doesn't get you the majority of dance students who just want a bit of fun, socialising and exercise. However a section of the market does want teachers with qualifications and wants to work towards dance medals. If this market is not catered for in your area then you might want to invest in a qualification.

REMEMBER: The dance teaching qualification will only be needed, by law, for teaching in publicly funded organisations.

STEP 4 - ADVERTISING

By now you should have done your market research and are ready to advertise. Advertising is not the same as marketing. Advertising is the way that you raise awareness of your product/service. In this case it is about raising awareness of your dance class in your area. A successful campaign reinforces your message and employs some or all of the following variety of methods.

REMEMBER: The first principle of advertising is to catch people's attention (so use bright colours and impacting images). The second principle of advertising is to then communicate your message in a way that is clear, simple and easy to understand and remember). The third principle of advertising is that there is no third principle because you've got to keep it simple.

Creating A Brand & Logo

A brand name sets the tone and aspirations for your class. Make a name and an image easy to "read" i.e. they are easy to understand with the type of dance form in its title e.g. "Salsa Style" or "Lindy Hop Movers" and the image a couple who are obviously dancing. The name of a location can also be included, to help people in finding your classes online e.g. Preston Swing Dance, but this may not have the same appeal as a more lyrical name. See the section on websites (in this STEP 4) for more about brand names.

It is important to also search the internet to make sure that brand is not already used by someone else. There is no copyright on a name unless it is trademarked – but creating your own name will avoid confusion and conflicts as well as showing that you are original.

You should then think of a strap-line of using in your advertising, e.g. "the coolest dance around." Also promote that dancing is fun, helps people make friends and helps them get fitter. The broader the appeal the more customers you will reach. However, don't make unrealistic claims and steer clear of saying customers will loose weight (so that those who come for that purpose don't feel self-conscious). Also include that your classes are for beginners and that they don't need to bring a partner.

Next you will need to put your brand and class details into some or all of the following advertising mediums.

Physical Advertising (Flyers, Posters, Banners etc)

Flyers, posters and banners should not contain too much information. Your flyers and posters should include a map if it is not an easy venue to find. The flyer should also have an image of the dance-floor if it is a good floor and you intend to take the flyers to dance events.

If you also make your flyers so that all the information can be read on one side then you can also use these as mini-posters if you put them on a shop notice board etc. See APPENDIX for Templates so that you can make sure that all the necessary information is there.

Posters – these can be left on the notice boards, walls and/or windows of supermarkets, sandwich bars, takeaways, cafes, charity shops. Always ask permission - mainly not to offend but also to prevent the poster being taken down straight away. See APPENDIX for Templates.

Flyers – these can be left at the same places as posters but also in your dance class and at large dance events (where there is already an interested market). See APPENDIX for Templates.

Banners/A-frames – these can be used outside your venue or on roads near to the venue and with a direction arrow. Make sure that they are securely fastened as loose banners are an invitation to vandals. A-frames should have less information than a banner as they are smaller. See APPENDIX for Templates.

Vehicle Livery – vehicle advertising can be used as when you are driving your vehicle around town this will increase your class visibility. You can make permanent changes to cars or can use temporary banners put in the windows and supported in place with cardboard sheet, boxes or sticks. You can also park these strategically on the main road arteries through town.

Be careful not to offend anyone with your parking as this will create bad advertising and always move if requested. Also be careful as vandals may damage your car and thieves steal your wheels. My favourite method is an A2 frame secured with nuts and bolts to a roof-rack (beware of car park entrances with this method).

Signs On Lamp-posts – these might be used as a last resort by the more anarchistic dance teachers to get the class going if their class does not have advertising on the main road. Whilst you may see a number of such adverts around these are not legal.

REMEMBER: Word of mouth is your best form of advertising.

Advertising In The Electronic Media (Websites, Facebook etc)

Websites – a website is your on-line shop front. It lends you credibility and is somewhere that you can direct customers who want more information. As with all advertising, keep it simple. To maximise on hits you need to consider how people will be web searching with key words for a dance class, and then repeat these key words on your home page.

".html" is a basic language for a website and the APPENDIX at the back has a version for you to copy. If you don't use ".html" then you can still see the kind of information to include in the APPENDIX.

Website Hosting And Domain Names - once you have built your website you can then find free web space on the internet (search for "Free Web Space") and upload your website to these. Once you have uploaded your website you can purchase a domain name that is easy to find if someone searches the location for a dance class e.g. to help bring traffic www.prestonsalsa.co.uk or www.prestonswingdance.co.uk.

If your brand name is not associated with the town e.g. "Sacred Salsa" or "Jazz Swing Dance" then you can have more than one domain name linking to the same site. This will increase your chances of hits. Web domains are cheap to buy but become more expensive to maintain after a couple of years (when the providers know they can charge more). So don't buy too many sites. You can also forward e-mails with the domain name e.g. info@jazzswingdance.co.uk into your e-mail account.

Facebook – social networking has become an important source of advertising, but whether this will continue (with the increase in dance teachers bombarding people with spam adverts) remains to be seen. The best source for advertising on social networks are customers who have friends and friends of friends who can recommend your class. You may need to keep active on Facebook and may not want to spend your evenings on the computer or to have your private life for all to see. If you want to keep your private life separate then you could set up separate Facebook accounts or find a friend who is happy to maintain your class presence on Facebook.

Facebook Groups – you can create Groups for friends to join and then you can message members of the group rather than spam friends. You can make these for dancers in your class and also for dancers in your region. If you create a general area group then you will be able to send everyone who joins the group (not just your friends) messages.

Facebook Events – you can create events when you have parties and then other friends can forward information about these events to their friends. At the events you can take photographs of customers who are also on Facebook, upload these into an album and then make links on the image to your customers. They will get a message that there is a photograph of them and a link. They will then be able to see themselves, reinforcing their sense of fun and belonging to your class. However make sure you get people's permission before you upload photographs of them (see photography section in this STEP 4).

Facebook Adverts – for a small bidding fee you can place adverts which you are only charged for in relation to the number of hits you get (and you can limit the amount you pay). This could be a good way to reach a broad market without directly approaching other teachers' Facebook friends. However, I don't know how effective these adverts are.

MySpace – sorry, I haven't used this but hear it is good for musicians and for music file sharing.

Twitter – sorry, I haven't used this but it is probably very useful.

New Media – keep your eye out for any new media or programme that is becoming widely adopted and learn how to use them. An integrated e-mail and texting system is supposed to be the next development (i.e. combining Facebook and Twitter).

Dance Listing Websites - search on-line to find dance classes or other services in your area and you will find a number of classes in online listing websites. List your class with them as they are good at getting customers who are searching the internet (as you will have just found). Make sure your details are there, particularly if other dance classes in your area are also there. Avoid paying a fee for any service.

Advertising In The Physical Media

Free Listings – check your local magazines and newspapers in the "What's On" section to see if you can put a free listing for your dance class. Make sure you have the right details for a contact at the newspaper/magazine. Telephone them if you are in doubt. Otherwise your listing may not get forwarded to the correct person.

Libraries and Tourist Information Centres – these often keep lists of local dance classes so make sure your are on their list. Visit, phone or e-mail them to find out if this list exists.

Telephone Directories - I've never included details in these as I avoid paying a fee but recognise it could be a good source.

Dance Industry Catalogues and Magazines - that you know will go to dancers of your dance form are worth considering at the right price – particularly if they also send you copies of the magazine that you can give away in your class. Work out how much the advert will cost, what its distribution numbers are, what its range is and how many more customers you are likely to get as a result.

Press Releases

So, you are ready to launch your dance class with friends and dancers. Get some free local publicity with a Press Release. Send this at least 2 weeks before the launch and ring up or visit your local paper to make sure that you have the correct contact. Ask them if you can get a reporter to come to the class with a photographer. The reporter might even be persuaded to do a feature of their experience learning to dance. To maximise on your chances of getting a photo in the paper you can also send a publicity photo of yourself. See APPENDIX for a SAMPLE PRESS RELEASE.

Publicity Photographs

It is important to spend time on your publicity photograph as it can be used for the press releases and on flyers, posters, websites and your Facebook site. Get a cheap but good quality digital camera (online, at a supermarket etc) and take a photograph of yourself and partner in dance clothing and standing in front of a coloured sheet. Make sure that the sheet fills the frame of the shot. A single colour background will make it easy to edit and change the background colour. Alternatively a simple background e.g. sky, fields or a wall, will not detract from the main subject of the photograph, the dancers.

Use a tripod or stand and a timer on your camera – unless you can get a friend/family to take the photo. You need to get your whole body into the shot (including feet and hands in styling positions). Choose a variety of poses. You can see what poses other images/clip art of dancers have used and then recreate the pose. Look at the camera and smile. Turn your bodies so that you are on display as the photo is about you. Take about 50 photos so that you can choose the best ones.

Make sure this is good quality and not too small or large a file size. Roughly 670 x 1000 pixels at 300dpi is good, as is 2304 x 3072 pixels at 72dpi. However you can always resize the picture and resend it if it is too large.

Lighting is important and photos outside in the sun have great light but be careful it is not behind you (have it shining on to your face instead) and be careful of shadows from the midday sun, or from your having to squint because you are looking into the sun. Get a cheap builder's/decorator's floodlight if you are taking the photo indoors, to help avoid shadows from the camera flash.

Take photos with and without flash so that you can choose the best ones. Crop the image to fit in the computer and touch up if you need to clean up the background.

Copyright Of Other Peoples Images

Taking your own photos means that you will have the copyright of your images and if you send a press release then you have a photo that they can instantly use. You can also use generic cartoons and free clip on your web site, flyers and posters although it is not good form (i.e. illegal) to use images of dancers without their permission (even if you see lots of other dance teachers doing this).

Permissions For Putting Images Of Dancers On-Line

Before taking photographs and videos at your class/event it is important to announce your intention to do this and to ask if anyone would object to your using images on your website, Facebook etc. It is bad form (i.e. illegal) to broadcast images of people without their permission and the internet (e.g. Youtube) is a broadcast media.

STEP 5 – YOUR CLASSES

Now that you have everything in place you can launch your classes and begin to create your success. This section is all about running your class. Here we will look at some issues that you will be able to decide upon before you begin teaching and other issues that you will need to decide upon as you go along.

Dance Partners

A dance partner is necessary for teaching complex moves.

A dance partner is also necessary if you want to split the class into 2 e.g. beginners and absolute beginners.

A dance partner is helpful so that one of you can take money whilst the other answers question, gives extra dance tips or makes customers feel at home. However, a dance partner is not absolutely necessary for these if you can juggle them. It is possible to run the class by yourself and receive all the takings. However you share the fun if you have a partner.

If your dance partner is your girlfriend/ wife/ boyfriend/ husband then if you break-up your relationship you will need to establish who the class (at that venue) belongs to. This is good to establish at the first instance if there is some ambiguity. Whose class your customers will want to patronise if you or your partner go to different venues is up to them.

Do You Teach Beginners Or Advanced?

The pros and cons of this question were discussed in the INTRODUCTION and should also have been partly answered by your market research. If there are lots of beginners classes then teach advanced. If there are lots of advanced classes then teach beginners. If there are no classes then you will need to teach beginners. If there are lots of both kinds of classes then maybe you should teach in another geographical area. If you are not an experienced dancers then start by teaching beginners.

Setting Up A Beginners Class

See the INTRODUCTION for more discussion of this. A main advantage is that you only need small number of dance moves to get going.

If you have a beginners class that gets too busy and the students don't want to keep going over the basics then split the class into 2 with an absolute beginners for new comers.

Eventually some of your students might want to take your students for an advanced class. You can't stop them and they will just turn people against you if you object. They wouldn't be setting up against you if aggression wasn't a part of their mindset. Be prepared for this and have a strategy to counter this.

If you did a good study of the venues in the area and chose the right venue in the first place then this will not be such a problem. However, now that your classes are a success then some of the venues that were not good, due to their bad location, will become possible because your class will be a potential "feeder" for these venues. Try not to become a "feeder" of anyone other than your own or a colleague's dance class. In the worst case scenario (of parasitic teachers poaching your customers) you may need to leave and set up somewhere else (see STEP 6).

Setting Up An Advanced Class

See the INTRODUCTION for more discussion of this. A disadvantage of this is that you will need more advanced moves so you need to be a good dancer before attempting an advanced class. Another disadvantage is that despite warning your beginner students they may not want to accept what their limitations are and may injure you, your customers and themselves if you are not careful. If you tell them that they shouldn't be doing the class then they may get resentful towards you.

Price

Charge at least the same price for doing a beginners class as an advanced class. Those doing an advanced class will get kudos and status but will also be benefiting from your hard work. So you should charge at least the same amount as you are doing a job that they cannot do (as often their egos and their need to be dance snobs will not permit it).

Don't think you are doing a service that dancers will be loyal over, they won't. Dance teaching isn't social work, it's business.

I had classes at £3.50 and £2.50 concessions only to find that retired and the unemployed customers would also be going to competitors classes priced at £5. I am an excellent dancer with lots of moves, shines, trick steps and styling but never used any of it in my classes because whenever dancers got to the point where they could learn advanced moves they were poached by less able teachers who were teaching just the more advanced moves and creating a climate to say that my classes were just for beginners.

So the lesson I learned was that to teach the beginners is the hardest thing to do, because you have to go over the same routines and never get the satisfaction of teaching the more advanced moves. So you should get the same or greater remuneration that the people who teach advanced.

REMEMBER: Eventually you may lose customers to those who teach only the more advanced moves. But the more dancers that you teach and pass on then the more will want to set up their own advanced classes (for the kudos and status). This means that they will then aggressively compete with each other, leaving you to look after the beginners.

Also people's perception of a cheaper class can be that it is not as good as a more expensive class (even if the teaching is better in the cheaper class). People get a level of satisfaction out of paying a higher amount for a product – as seen in the buying of designer fashion.

If you would like to keep the price down, but still want the perception of an exclusive price, then you can use Club cards or offer a free class for every 5 classes. Club cards become a form of advertising and reminders held within a person's pocket and create a sense of belonging. A Club card works in that the customer pays a small yearly fee so that they are then on a reduced weekly rate. Some will come back and take advantage of this and others will not. In which case those who buy the Club card but never come back balance out the discount that you give your regulars.

Some dancers begin to feel that they are doing you a favour by coming to your classes and expect to be allowed to dance for free. You have to decide if they are doing you a favour or not. If they dance with everyone, regardless of ability and looks then this can be a good idea. However, if they come to cream off you best customers then this creates a non-sharing environment. At the worst case they may also have come to try to persuade your best dancers to go to other classes so charging them will help prevent them from doing this by making them respect the service you provide.

Teaching Attitude & Tone Of The Class

Enjoy your teaching and keep it relaxed and fun.

Add humour and get dancers to introduce themselves to each other as they move around the class.

Add the occasional please and thank you when asking customers to do things in the class.

Encourage people to dance with each other and suggest that people should always agree to at least one dance when asked/invited.

Praise your dancers (individually and as a group) for the progress that they are making.

Dress smart to set the standard of professionalism and so that people can dress up or down as much as they like.

**Dancing In The Middle With Partner
vs Dancing With Students**

Dancing in the middle with just your partner helps to show people the moves before they learn them. It can create a perception of coldness but also allows you to be seen as a professional. Dancing in the middle with the students is helpful with easy moves but can be difficult when wanting to demonstrate complicated moves. Dancing with the students can also create a perception that you are not as good and professional.

Whether you dance with students in the middle or not, you should still make sure that you help them in the practice dancing. The students do not always count your dancing with them in the middle as you helping them. So for them to feel you are helping them you need to dance with them after the lesson as well.

Encouraging Couples To Move Around

Encourage people to move around but allow couples to stay together if they express a preference – even if you know they will not learn as effectively (as they will not get the benefit of practicing with better dancers).

REMEMBER – the dance class is not just about the dancing. It is social as well. Make sure that couples feel comfortable about staying together if they want to. Suggest to the whole group that couples can stay together as the couples may feel to shy to ask.

Bonding With Customers

Bonding with customers will give you their loyalty and is a natural result of your providing them with a service that they are happy with. However, when something else comes along that is of more appeal then they will often see you as just a service provider (rather than the loyal friend that you thought they were) and go off. To avoid disappointment don't expect too much from your students. That way you will be delighted when they treat you as more than just a service provider.

Good service is expected by customers and almost taken for granted. However, bad service or a single incident can be a source of disproportionate dissatisfaction that can lead to a build up of resentment. It can also break the bond that you have taken years to build up. To prevent this you should encourages customers to share feedback.

Customers do not always offer feedback so try and show them that you listen to all feedback, that you don't take it personally and then try to change things to satisfy them or explain to them why you can't change things.

Identify what each customer wants from the class and try to provide that for them. However, don't spend too much time with demanding customers. They rarely give back in loyalty once they have what they want. Make sure you look after everyone.

Learn people's names. Show an interest in them and listen to them rather than talk at them. Smile at people and look them in the eye.

Outings to dance events, party nights and meals/Jacobs joints are all some of the ways you can help create a friendly loyalty from your customers. However, only do these if you want to do them. As you need to be yourself and any discomfort might come across as unfriendliness.

Provide people with links to music, shoes and clothes to make it easier for them to get involved in the dancing culture. Approach local dance shoe and clothes shops and put their flyers out as they put yours out.

Use social media, like Facebook, to add photos from dance nights and students will put links on photos to each other names and message each other about the night, as well as creating their own links and networks. Remember to check with people before taking their photos and uploading them online.

WARNING: If you do not bond with your customers then your competitors will take advantage of this and bond with them so they can poach them. It is important you start teaching in an area where you fit socially and there are people you like, otherwise it will go against the grain and your customers will be taken from you.

Core Dancers

Build a solid core of dances. Don't worry if you only get 1 regular dancer for every 10 that come to the class. If you get 5 new dancers a week then that will be 25 regulars after 1 year and this is in addition to the occasional dancers that you will be getting. Listen to what these customers want from the class and try to deliver this for them.

Don't worry too much about attracting university students as they are only temporary (term-time) and will be there for only 3 years (unless studying locally to their parental home).

Goal Setting

Have social events and nights that people can work towards. People will want to practice so that they can get ready for an event. The event may be one that you host at your own venue or may be an event outside the area that people can travel to. If the event is at your venue this may also bring in other dancers from around the area.

BEWARE: you may lose your dancers to poachers at these events but if you have the best venue then this is not a problem.

BEWARE: setting an event as a goal may also lose your dancers as soon as they have met that goal – e.g. a Valentine's event after New Year can lose a large number of dancers who will feel they have met a goal. At the same time you may have lost them earlier if they had not felt that they had a goal to work towards.

Program Of Dance Moves

Creating a program of dance moves (formally as a list for the students or informally in your head) helps to create a standard set of moves that students can practice with each other and this enables them to dance socially with each other sooner. You can also put the moves on Youtube and/or encourage students to film you (or themselves) doing the moves on their mobile phones to help them remember the moves.

The program will help your students learn, but be wary of giving this list to your students else they think that they have already learned the moves and get bored with the moves too soon. They need to feel spontaneity in the class so you can list a few key moves to help them but always teach extra moves that are not on the list.

If you teach too well it is satisfying but the customer will take the credit and will not put it down to your teaching. If you teach badly then they will blame you (unless you are a "wolf pack leader" (see STEP 6) who blames them and creates a climate of fear in your class – not an advisable thing to be).

Youtube Movies

If you make instructional films then use your own music then if you get lots of hits Youtube will pay you royalties. Put your best Youtube movie on your website to increase traffic. However, also manage the comments on your films. If people leave negative comments then this can damage confidence in your class.

Dancing Demonstrations

Respond to requests for demonstrations occasionally in your class or at your events. If you do these then try to include tricks and dips as the audience will expect this (particularly as expectations have been raised following Strictly Come Dancing). Without these special moves your audience may begin to get bored or feel that you have stopped them from dancing for no good reason.

Choose a track that has popular appeal (but not one that everyone has been waiting to dance to) and that lasts for just 2½ to 3½ minutes. Leave the audience wanting more, not less. End in a difficult trick pose or hold.

Don't do demonstrations too often or you might be accused of showing off.

Congresses & Being The Best

With your program of dance moves, your Youtube movies and your dancing demonstrations you may begin to feel like your dancing is really going places. However, keep your eye on the ball. Don't worry about being the best dancer in the world or being invited to teach at Congresses. Concentrate on being one of the best teachers in your area. And remember that being a good teacher is not just what you teach in the lesson but also about all the other aspects of setting up and running a dance class (as outlined in this book).

Concentrate on keeping your customers happy. The best dancers often have small, select classes as they neglect the teaching of beginners as they don't always have the patience or interest to teach them, even though they are the main customer of dance teaching. As a result the best dancers need income streams from DVD sales, from private teaching and corporate events.

Competitions

Audience judging makes these easily achievable. Buy a small, cheap (but photogenic) trophy and medals from a trophy shop. Don't worry about engraving them unless it is going to be a big event as the engraving is the most expensive cost. Then take these to the event with a coloured table cloth to display them on. Give customers a slip of paper on entry to the event.

The contestants all get on the floor at the same time and dance to 3 tracks. Then the couples are lined up and each is given an A4 sheet with a number. Customers then write their favoured number down and put their votes in a box.

Music is played whilst the votes are counted. Tie breaks are decided with a dance-off. The finalists then stand with their numbers and customers are given new slips of paper to cast a new vote (or are just asked for a show of hands). Finally, bronze, silver and gold medals are awarded along with the trophy and photographs are taken.

This is another way to get the local press involved. You can get press coverage both in advance of the event and if you take a good photo of the winners with their medals also as a follow up to the event. You can also add images of the winners to your website and Facebook.

Open Air Events

Your local park or seaside promenade can be a great venue for free open air promotional events. Find a spot that you think is suitable. Check to make sure the dance area will be suitable for normal shoes as most people will not bring dance shoes (let people know if dance shoes will not be suitable). Contact your council to get permission and a date (print the letter to show any wardens on the day). You will probably need a small generator and a music system loud enough to drown out the generator and to counter any wind. Also arrange an alternative venue in case of rain.

Weddings

Sometimes customers will request that you help them get ready for their wedding dance and that you also teach and do a demonstration at the evening reception. Often they will not come back after the wedding but if you have helped their big day be a success then that is reward enough (as well as your fee). There are a few points to note to help make such events a success.

The main thing is to remember that the wedding is about them and their family, not you and your dancing. So before you do any demonstration at the event make sure that you emphasise how hard the couple have worked at their dancing (they will have done), how good they have progressed and what a great couple they make.

After you demo people may feel too intimidated to get up and dance, so promise to teach them something very easy – that takes 5 minutes to learn or can be learn as you go along. The wedding couple want you to help their guests have fun so Merengue or Charleston stomp are good dances to teach.

When people have learnt a fun dance then you can try and get all the guest involved in a dance like the Conga. However, it is worth learning some basic Conga moves before attempting this – so you have something to show the guests that they don't already know how to do.

If you want the event to go really well then don't worry about your credibility as a dance teacher and what good moves you can teach (unless lots and lots of dancers are at the wedding). You will show you are good teacher by the event going well and everyone having fun.

Holidays

You will now have earned yourself a rest. Upon announcing your holiday plans to your dancers one or two of them may request that they run the class whilst you are away. Be careful of letting them do this unless you trust them as they may then use it as an opportunity to begin their own class and set up somewhere else. It happens. To avoid this you might want to plan you holidays around traditional holiday periods Christmas and August (when class numbers are down due to people looking after children or away on holiday themselves).

Alternatively you can embrace the fact that they want to set up a class and work with them, helping them with advice and making announcements for them. Be careful that this will be appreciated and reciprocated. And make sure everyone knows that you are helping them so that they can make no claims that you were hindering them at a later date.

LESSON TEMPLATE

1. First Lesson (1 hour)

1a. Footwork Warm up

1b. Teach the moves. Begin with some easy moves then introduce the week's new move(s). Rotate dancers to move onto the next partner (usually ladies move round anti-clockwise) and get everyone to introduce themselves to their new partners. Teach with a partner in the middle or just by yourself by taking a new partner each time you rotate partners. Play slow music until everyone gets the moves and then medium music.

2. Practice Dancing (30 minutes)

2a. Customers dance with each other whilst the teacher takes payment from the customers. The teacher can also ask new customers to sign the Visitors book and add their e-mail address or other contact details. If there is time the teacher dances with the customers.

2b. The customers should also be encouraged to practice in a group dance . Starting with 1 couple, they dance their new learned routines for about 30 seconds and then split to applause and take new partners. The 2 couples dance for about 30 seconds and split so there are 4 couples, then 8 couples etc. The benefit of this is that everyone dances together and bonds as a group. It encourages shy people to get up dance and gets the dance-floor full and busy.

3. Second Lesson (45 minutes)

3a. Footwork Warm up

3b. Teach the moves. Begin with some standard moves then introduce the new move(s). Rotate dancers to move onto the next partner. Play slow music until everyone gets the moves and then medium music.

4. Practice Dancing.

Customers dance with each other and the teacher chases up any final payments from the customers. The teacher dances with the customers.

STEP 6 – STAYING SUCCESSFUL

Being A Success May Be The Start Of Your Problems

Now that your class is up and running and a complete success you may find that you become subject to the "Butcher's Shop Syndrome". This is where one butcher opens a shop on the high street and his business is a success. Soon after another butcher opens, then another, and another. Before too long you have 4 butchers on one street, all catering for the same number of people and all making less profit.

At this point you need to ask yourself if you should stay and battle with the other butchers/dance teachers or just start somewhere else. After all, if you followed the principles in this book starting up should be easy for you now – and you will have become a leader and a trend setter – so spread your wings. You may find an even better dance venue and dance form out there just waiting for you.

Staying One Step Ahead

If you want to stay ahead then it is advisable to look at your product (dance style) curves. Develop the next product before the market reaches its peak with the current product. If there is a saturation of teachers providing your dance form then look to see what the next dance craze is likely to be. However, the idea is that you should try to identify national trends and not just your own preferences.

To stay ahead is also the best way to avoid the poachers (see "wolves" below). The majority of people struggle with learning more than one style of dance and so most of the time like to stick to one style (although occasionally they like to learn other dance styles so that they feel like they are capable of dancing lots of dance styles). If you begin teaching a new dance style then the poachers will not be able to take your customers as easily unless they change their classes. They won't do this because their egos will be invested in their own dance class. You will have a couple of years of grace before the whole process begins again and other people see the success of your dance classes and decide that they will change their style.

This book helps give you the skills to be either a trend setter or a trend follower with your setting up of a dance class. You can wait to see a dance style established in an area and then set up when you know that that dance form works, or you can go out on a limb. The principles are the same. Just make sure you are catering for what the market (dancers) wants. And make sure you work respectfully and co-operatively with other dance teachers.

The Psychology Of Dancers

To explore the psychology of dancers we're going to begin with using an analogy of how dancers can be separated into sheep and wolves or dolphins and sharks. This is an analogy and it is not advisable to actually think of dancers as sheep. Think of them more as like dolphins. However, we will use the sheep/wolf analogy as it is about seeing yourself as being like a shepherd/ shepherdess who offers the dancers a level of protection and in return they follow you knowing that you will look after them. However, it is also easy for other teachers to lead them astray.

There are those who dance for fun: sheep (dolphins)

There are those who teach dance: shepherds

There are those who take dancing too seriously. They will dance their way to the top and then do the same with their dance teaching: wolves (sharks)

The teacher must decide if they want to be a shepherd or the lead wolf in a pack of wolves.

In your class of sheep there will be a number of wolves who will be more tenacious and ambitious. A shepherd can cater for wolves up to a point then ask them to leave if they are too unpleasant.

You can't shepherd wolves, the only way to deal with them is to have the best venue and the best visibility for that venue. This will defend you against their attacks. So if you set up with the right venue this will maintain your stability.

Work with other shepherds and always offer the hand of friendship to wolves in case they have a change of heart.

If there are too many wolves in an area then it may be time to go elsewhere or begin a new dance form.

The sheep and wolves analogy can be useful but doesn't want to be extended too far – particularly as the shepherd fleeces the sheep and sends the lambs for slaughter. We will return to it later, after we have continued in our psychological investigation by looking at Abraham Maslow's Hierarchy of Needs.

This model is a pyramid of motivators, at the bottom of which are Physiological needs, then when these are met Safety needs are considered, then Love and Belonging, then Self-Esteem and finally Self-Actualization.

Translated into dance requirements this means that at the bottom level your Physiological needs have to be met e.g. with a warm environment. On the next level the Safety needs e.g. of a good dance-floor, with drinks available and with good parking outside, all have to be met. On the next level there needs to be a feeling that your class provides an emotionally safe environment, where the teacher likes you and where there won't be aggressive and condemnatory behaviours. In this level the students will need to feel that they are Loved, Belong and can have fun. Further up they will need to feel that their Self-Esteem can increase. Finally they need to feel that the class will help them to become who they really are.

The problem with such a situation is that for some dancers Self-Actualisation becomes feeling superior to other dancers, thus undermining the Safe environment that beginning dancers need in the first place. So you can end up teaching people who will eventually undermine your classes.

Unfortunately you can't control what gives people their senses of self-esteem and self-actualisation. It may be that becoming a good dancer replaces other insecurities that they feel. It may be their personality naturally gravitates to arrogance. To explore this further we will look at another model of motivation.

According to Frederick Herzberg's Motivation-Hygiene Theory people are influenced by two sets of factors. "Motivator Factors" relate to motivational activities that are carried out and "Hygiene Factors" relate to the environment that is required for these to be carried out.

Dancers can be motivated by "Motivator Factors" in relation to their actual dancing - like their achievements of learning in the lesson, their improvements as dancers and the recognition they are given for this. But if the "Hygiene Factors" are not satisfied then the dancer will not be satisfied and will not be motivated. So before you can effectively motivate dancers you need to remove all the sources of dissatisfaction.

People are made dissatisfied by a bad environment, but are not made satisfied by a good environment. In a dance context these "Hygiene Factors" would include the conditions of dance venue, the customer's status in the dance class, and their personal relationship with other dancers.

Another way of looking at this is that there are core conditions that must exist before motivation can occur. In dance class terms they are the features that a class must have so that people do not complain, e.g. a bar, good dance floor, good music and parking. Once these conditions have been met then the motivators of having fun and learning to dance come into play. So don't think that you are working for your dancers by providing the bar, good dance floor, good music and parking. These are all just necessary for you to begin teaching the dancers and the teaching is the only work they recognise your having done. However, subconsciously if you provide all these necessary things then I believe that you will still be seen as a better teacher by the students.

Now, if we extend this further then even the dance teaching may be seen as a "Hygiene Factor" for some customers. They are moving through degrees of dissatisfaction until their prime motivator (of being a good dancer and showing off) is allowed to appear. This explains why dancers often show little loyalty to teachers.

So the only way to manage their need to set up in direct competition with you is to manage their progression and trying to instil a dance ethos in them as they progress. And you can do this by listening to customers, encouraging them to dance with less able dancers, and if there are requests for extra classes (that you can't do) then offer to help people set up and work together and recommend to them the reading of this book. Co-operation is the key.

SECRETS:

Don't worry about dancers being better than you.

Don't worry about dancers setting up against you.

Don't worry about dancers poaching customers.

Just make sure that you have the biggest and the best dance-floor in your area.

Make sure that you have the best venue.

Make sure that you look after the beginners.

Now to return to the sheep and wolves analogy with the knowledge that aggressive dancers can't help being aggressive, any more than wolves can't help being wolves. The ones that you can influence are the sheep in wolves' clothing, and, if you are lucky, the wolves in sheep's clothing

The wolves will always come looking for new sheep and acting like wolves in sheep's clothing. A way to undermine them is to point out to them and your customers (at the same time) what they are attempting. To let everyone know that you have offered to work with them but that they seem to have temporarily lost their scruples, possibly due to their arrogance or due to taking the dancing too seriously. Sheep will agree with you, wolves will side with them. However, if you highlight this to your sheep it will, at least show you are a strong leader and it will make them aware of what is happening so that they are less likely to be tricked into going elsewhere and into becoming sheep in wolves clothing. Others will readily become wolves themselves. The next section on "Dirty Tricks" helps you be aware of them.

Dirty Tricks

If you have turned to this section with glee then you will probably be disappointed as you will no doubt be able to think of far dirtier tricks than those that follow. For the rest of readers it is a sad fact that whilst aggressive people are a minority of the population they often get what they want by shouting the loudest. However, getting what you want by breaking etiquette is not to be confused with success.

Just as there is an etiquette in dancing (e.g. always have at least one dance with a person when they ask you, or don't blame your partner if they are not dancing properly) so also there is etiquette in inter-teacher relations. The following have not been done by any persons know to me so the fictional teachers described bear no resemblance to any persons know to me. I put them here so that you are aware that theoretically there are unscrupulous people out there. If you consider doing any of these tricks then please don't.

Negativity

Even if you are polite and helpful to your customers for years and you never say a bad word about other teachers if other people (or even your customers) set up against you then they may find that they begin to invent reasons to criticise you both professionally and personally. They may start aggressively criticising (slagging off) your teaching, music and dance-floor. They might even team up with other teachers to attack you.

They can take the smallest things and blow them out of proportion, changing their criticisms to suit their current state of mind or dance experience. Even if you were to change your music, lessons, dance-floor, venue etc to counter their criticism they still wouldn't come. Furthermore they will project any criticisms that they think might fall on themselves back onto you – such as saying you are not a nice person even when you have always been pleasant to everyone, including them.

If they were polite people then they would be trying to work with you rather than setting up on the same nights and fighting for the same customers. They would have come and spoken with you about co-operating. However, even if you try and co-operate the chances are they won't be interested and will just misinterpret you intention of peacemaking as sarcasm.

They can also get dance teaching qualification and then use them to criticise you if you are without one. Unfortunately, whilst professional dance organisations teach that you shouldn't criticise other qualified dance teachers as part of business ethics they leave out that they shouldn't criticise unqualified dance teachers.

Finally, not content with criticising another teacher's dancing and teaching, some teachers end up criticising another teacher's personal life, family, and outside professions. And they even get other people (their customers and your ex-customers) to do the criticisms (and gossip) for them, so that they are not seen to be doing it personally.

However, don't worry about them. Just get on with your own being helpful and pleasant to customers. If it gets so that it will affect your personal or family life then walk away. Don't see it as them winning or being a success. To behave like this is to be a failure. They will have destroyed all the good atmosphere that you have created but they will also probably destroy themselves with infighting in the end. The best thing is to not waste energy on them and to let them destroy themselves. Just move on somewhere else that you can have the best venue with the nicest people.

Undermining Students

Some teachers create a climate of fear and anxiety in students about their not being good enough. It is a way of bullying students (part of the wolf pack mentality) by shouting at them in the class to humiliate them and undermine their self-confidence and their confidence in other teachers. The bully teacher then promises that only they can fulfil the student's dance class needs (e.g. asserting that only they teach in the correct way).

They also make the competitor teacher out to be the enemy and a scapegoat figure so that the bullied student is quick to turn against the competitor. They join the wolf pack and unite against a common enemy rather than have the bullying teacher focus that aggression upon them. And they put up with this because they think that they can find their self-actualisation through the aggressive teacher, i.e. deep down they aspire to be like this.

Poaching Customers

Whilst it is natural for dancers to exchange details and recommendations about other classes some competitors send dancers to deliberately and systematically poach dancers from your class by chatting and flyering (often targeting the new customers). Doing this covertly rather than asking your permission is an aggressive action that shows a lack of respect to you as a teacher.

This poaching isn't a problem if there are good relations between classes and the exchange of flyers is all part of co-operation. But if competitors are being negative about you then it is problematic as you will not want your customers to be exposed to their aggressive comments. You may need to confront the poachers and politely put it to them, in a positive way, that you are trying to build a class and that it would be really good that any promoting about other classes in your class can be reciprocated by their promoting your class in the other classes. If they are giving out flyers then you can even give them a handful of your flyers to take (though insist that they ask before putting them out at the competitor's class).

If they persist poaching in subsequent weeks then talk to them again to check that they have also promoted your class at your competitors. If they haven't then suggest that if they persist in promoting your competitors but are not prepared to promote you to an equal degree, then it might be a good idea for them to stop coming to your classes.

Another for of this poaching is by using e-mail addresses in the cc when other teachers send them e-mails (I confess I did this once for a regional event and got a couple of abusive e-mails as a result) or by sending friend invites to all a competitor's friends on Facebook.

Gazumping

It is good to be aware that the following methods of gazumping are used.

You may find that some teachers set up on the same night in the same area as you and advertise in all the same places without speaking to you (or other teachers) first. In large cities with lots of classes going on then this is normal but in small towns with just one or two classes then it is better to work together with other teachers.

You may find that a teacher approaches a venue that already runs a competitors class and tries to arrange to do a class on another night without talking to the competitors first.

An exception to this being a dirty trick is if your competitors have a history of aggression toward you and have deliberately set up at a large venue (one that you previously approached but was not viable without you setting up other classes) and will be parasitic on your classes by poaching your customers to make their class work.

If you know they will be hostile to you and it was a venue you were working towards having then you should just approach the venue direct. This is not a dirty trick, it is a counter to a dirty trick.

However if the manager talks with them and they are not willing to share, despite their using your class as a feeder for theirs and you can't find an alternative large venue, then you may need to leave the area. Hence the importance of setting up in the best venues in the first place – although these may not be viable until you have got the dancing scene going in smaller venues.

Finally, you may find that some teachers approach a venue that already runs a competitor's class and tells the owner that they can get more people if they take over the class.

Knowing When To Quit

A final irony of being a success is that you also need to know when to quit and/or retire. So if your class is not building after 6 months due to having no market interest, or you have competitors taking your students, or the wolves are getting too unpleasant, then it may be time to change venue and/or area. Don't be afraid to recognise when your classes are not working and be prepared to move on. Nothing lasts for ever and if your class in a venue lasts for more than a few years you are doing very well.

It is important to be flexible in the marketplace. A "teacher" is not just themselves and their abilities, they are partly their venue. However, on the other hand a teacher is not just their venue. They are a brand and a person who can take their class to another venue and town and make a success of it there (following the principles in this book).

Remember that you can always return to dance teaching at a future date. And your competitors will either be caretakers of the dancing scene in your area until you return or they will have destroyed the dancing scene and people will be ready for you to return with your fun and friendly dance classes.

APPENDIX

POSTER/ FLYER/BANNER TEMPLATE

IMAGES
Imageofdancers.jpeg
Imageofdancefloor.jpeg (not needed on poster or banner)
Map.jpeg (not needed on a banner)

LARGE STYLISED BOLD FONT
Dance Form: **Swing Dance**

LARGE BOLD FONT
Day: **MONDAYS** Town: **Preston**

SMALLER FONT
Time: 7.30pm
Price: £5
Venue: Masonic Hall
Postcode: PR1 2QU
Age range: 18+
Contact: Anthony & Stephanie 0790 2342448
Website: www.jazzswingdance.co.uk
Class details (not needed on banner):
    Beginners 7.30pm, Improvers 8.30pm, Dancing 9.30pm - late

EXTRA ITALICISED (Not Needed On Small Banner)
Strapline: *The coolest dance around*
Encouragement: *Absolute Beginners Welcome*
No partner needed.
Benefits: *Have fun, get fit and make friends*

A-FRAME (OUTSIDE VENUE) TEMPLATE

IMAGES
Imageofdancers.jpeg

LARGE STYLISED BOLD FONT
Dance Form: **Swing Dance**

LARGE BOLD FONT
Day: **MONDAYS**
Time: **7.30pm**

LARGE FONT
Venue: Masonic Hall
Contact: 0790 2342448

LARGE ITALICISED FONT
Strapline: *Learn 2 Dance*

WEBSITE TEMPLATE

A basic website can be created with the following Website Template – change the text in italics to fit you, your class, brand etc, and take it out of italics. Insert appropriate images and change the names of the images (use lower case). Save as small Jpegs (maz 600 pixels wide). Past all text onto a notepad document and then save in a folder as "all files" and type .html behind the file name.

Put all the images you are using in the website within the same folder, so that they show up on the website. When completed you will need to upload the .html page and images to some free web-space (search on-line for this) and then get a domain name to link that webpage.

<html><head>
<title> *SALSA/SWING* dancing lessons in *TOWN, COUNTY, REGION, COUNTRY*</title>
<meta http-equiv="Keywords" name="Keywords" content=" *SALSA/SWING*, Dancing, Learn, Lessons, TOWN, COUNTY, REGION, COUNTRY">
<meta http-equiv="Description" name="Description" content=" *SALSA/SWING*, Dancing, Learn, Lessons, TOWN, COUNTY, REGION, COUNTRY">
</head><body bgcolor="red">
<table border="0" width="600" align="center"><tr><td>
<font color="white"><center>

<b><p><img src=" *dancers*.jpg"alt="Welcome" width="600"><br clear="all"></p>

```
<p><center><h3>With YOUR NAME and PARTNER'S
NAME</h3></p>

<p><center><h2>Welcome.<br>Looking for
SALSA/SWING dance in TOWN?
 <br><b><img src="logo.jpg"alt="YOUR BRAND
NAME" width="300">

<br>We are one of the friendliest <br>SALSA/SWING
dance clubs<br>in TOWN and the REGION.</p>
<p>We give you the basics of the SALSA/SWING dance
so that you can be up and dancing at any SALSA/SWING
dance event. </h2></p>

<br><h1><p><center>WEEKLY CLASSES</p>
<p>DAY<br>VENUE<br>ADDRESS WITH
POSTCODE.</a></p></h1>

<h2><p>Beginners SALSA/SWING 7.30pm <br>Practice
dancing 8.15pm
<br><br>Beginners SALSA/SWING 8.30pm
<br>Practice dancing  9.30pm - late<br></p>
<p><img src="dancefloor.jpg"alt="the dancefloor"
width="450"><br clear="all"></p>
<p>Superb venue with bar.</p>
<p><img src="map.jpg"alt="How to find us"
width="600"><br clear="all"></p>
<p><br>No partner needed.<br>Dress - smart or
casual.<br>18+</p></h2>

<h1>PRICE £5 - for both lessons and dancing.</h1>
<h2>(£2.50 - for just practice dancing)</h2>
```

\<img src="*email address and phone number*.jpg"alt="Contact Us" width="450"\>\<br clear="all"\>

\<p\>\<img src="*teachers*.jpg"alt="Your Teachers" width="200"\>\<br clear="all"\>
\<h3\>\<p\>*YOUR NAME* has been dancing for *X* years. YOUR NAME* has *QUALIFICATIONS* \</p\>
\<p\>*PARTNER'S NAME* has been dancing for *X* years. PARTNER'S NAME* has *QUALIFICATIONS* \</p\>\</h3\>

\<h1\>Link\</h1\>
\<h2\>\<p\>\<img src="*colleague*.jpg"alt="Other Classes/Events" width="500"\>\<br clear="all"\>\</p\>
\<p\>\<a href="http://www.*COLLEAGUE WEBSITE*"\>Click here for *COLLEAGUE*.\</a\> \<br\>A fantastic *SALSA/SWING* Dance night, at the *VENUE NAME, TOWN, COUNTY*.\</p\>\</h3\>\</b\>\</center\>\</h2\>

\</font\>\</td\>\</tr\>\</table\>\</body\>\</html\>

SAMPLE PRESS RELEASE

PRESS RELEASE – For Immediate Attention

WHAT: "Launch Of New Swing Dance Class" By Local Dance Teachers

WHEN: 1st August 2010, 7.30pm-10.30pm

WHERE: Masonic Hall, Saul Street, Preston, PR1 2QU

CONTACT: Anthony Padgett 0790 2342448
info@jazzswingdance.co.uk

Anthony Padgett is a North West based dance teacher and, along with his partner Stephanie, he is launching a new Swing dance class in Preston. The classes are aimed at Absolute Beginners. So everyone is welcome and no partner is needed. The Beginners lessons start at 7.30pm and cost just £5. The Age range is 18+

A quote from you is always good as it makes the paper look like it has sent a journalist to interview you.

Anthony says "There has been a real resurgence of interest in all things vintage and we think that Swing Dance is the coolest dance around. It's a great way to have fun, to get fit and to make friends. This is the first time a class like this has started in Preston so we are really excited as it is very popular all around the UK. So with the ever increasing popularity of dance on shows like Strictly Come Dancing we hope to see the classes go from strength to strength."

A bit of historical information about the dance helps the reader to relate to it more.

Swing dance is a mixture of the Charleston from the 1920's, the Lindy Hop from the 1930's and the Jive from the 1940's. It covers music from the Jazz era, through the wartime Big Band sounds of Glenn Miller, all the way to the 1950's Crooners like Frank Sinatra, Dean Martin and Sammy Davis Junior.

For further information contact Anthony on 0790 2342448 or visit the class website www.jazzswingdance.co.uk

96

ALSO AVAILABLE BY THE SAME AUTHOR

MURDER AT THE MIDLAND HOTEL
Murder on the Dance Floor No.1
ISBN 978-0-9561587-5-8
The first novella in a series of Murder on the Dance Floor mysteries. Rachel Foxe is called to investigate a missing husband and finds a deadly web of intrigue and deceit in a Charleston and Lindy Hop dance at Morecambe's famous Art Deco Midland Hotel.

SALSA MOST FOUL
Murder on the Dance Floor No.2
ISBN 978-0-9561587-6-5
The second novella in a series of Murder on the Dance Floor mysteries. Rachel Foxe is on a Salsa Dance holiday in Havana, Cuba, when a young dancer is found, ritually murdered, exposing the darkest heart of the Salsa Dance craze.

TALES FROM THE OLD COFFEE HOUSE
ISBN 978-0-9561587-8-9
23 tales from 23 regions of coffee production. Each story designed to be read in the time it takes to drink a cup of coffee. Each story with a surprising flavour. Set off from Atkinsons Old Coffee House on a journey around the world.